JUDITH

G WOLF

TIDBITS

AGAIN

2 Acknowledgement

Another huge thank you to George Susich, Creative Director at Susich Design Co. for putting this book together, to Chris Loomis for wonderful photography, to Alicia Keenon for suggestions and proofreading, and to Lee Ann Grace for a great job proofreading this book.

Cover / Book Design: Susich Design Co, Phoenx AZ
Back Image: Chris Loomis
978-0-9967860-8-9

Judith G. Wolf, Ph.D. is a poet and promoter of the arts. Her published poetry collections include *Weeping Shadows, Tidbits, Otherwise, Tidbits Two* and *I Hate Being in Love Alone*. In addition to Poems of Life (twelve poems from *Otherwise*, Composer Kenneth Fuchs, première April 8, 2017, Virginia Symphony Orchestra recorded at Abbey Road as part of a four selection recording of Fuchs' music, which won a Grammy in February 2019), Wolf's poetry has been set to music by composers Clint Borzoni (*Father's Song*, première May 2023, Phoenix, Arizona and *Tidbits*, première February 2017, Belvedere, California), Persis Vehar (*Random Thoughts*, première May 2023, Phoenix, Arizona) and (*Life, Love, Timelessness*, première January 2012, Albuquerque, New Mexico), Michael Lewis (*Fresh Grief*, première Chandler, Arizona December 2018) and Mason Bates (*Afterlife*, première Phoenix Symphony, January 2013). Wolf founded Arizona Spark, which supports the development and production of innovative new operatic works for Arizona Opera. She also cofounded the Phoenix Symphony Commissioning Club, which commissioned Kenneth Fuchs to write *Quiet in the Land*, first performed by the orchestra in March 2018. Wolf's diverse educational and professional background includes a Ph.D. in Educational Psychology, a master's degree in Elementary and Remedial Education, and far-reaching experience in arts administration. She serves on several boards of directors including Arizona Opera, the HonorHealth Foundation, The Metropolitan Opera Laffont Competition (President of the Board) and is a member of Rotary 100. Wolf cofounded Young Arts Arizona Ltd., a nonprofit art organization that serves at-risk children by exhibiting their artwork and teaching art to children not served by other organizations. She is a Reiki master and a Doctor of Ministry through the Universal Life Church. For complete information, see: judithgwolf.com

JUDITH

G. WOLF

TIDBITS

AGAIN

What will I do without you?
Who will inspire me to write
nasty poetry?

6

No poem here
not even a sneeze
drips off the quill.

It's unnerving to know you are
the oldest person at the entire
rock concert.

8 Intimacy is your ass and mine
sharing the same toilet seat.

I whisper platitudes,
pleasantries to no one
in particular.

10   Every time I hear from you
        I smile.

When I am not with you
I am tomorrow waiting
for the next hug.

12   If I knew this would be
      the last time we made love
      I might have paid more attention.

My Nana sat with her hands on her cheeks pulling up the years.

14   If you text me when you're on the
toilet it shouldn't take up
any extra time.

Are you still asleep or did you just
forget about me?

Leap into love
do not pass go
do not ask Mother May I.

If you think about us
like a sitcom it works.

18

If you have to pass gas
don't do it while wearing
an oil cloth raincoat.

Oh is that the vibration from the ship starting? I thought it was because I am sitting next to you.

I'll remember this scenario.
You by my side not a word
of neglect.

Best trip ever.
No wet toilet seats.

22

You've had a lot to drink.
Do you like me now?

Was it a 10 goose bump
kind of event?

24   Being with you is like playing a
fine violin carefully with vigor.

Lonely finger

sits on my hand wondering.

I am afraid
I won't live up to my résumé.

He has more personalities
than I do.

28   Love is a semicolon.

I love him he doesn't love me
he loves me I don't love him
I don't even love myself.
It's a sad situation.

30   Love and honesty are valued above all else. How do you add up?

My hand is like an anatomy lesson.
Veins and sinews.

I just want you to hold me
so I can cry.

Grief follows you around
like a mosquito. Every once
in a while it takes a drink.

34 You left on a dime
not even a wave.
Dreams depart.

In the night the ghost sits on
my lap telling stories.

36   I have so many conversations with
you when you're not around.

It's a lot of work being a widow.
Exhausting really.

They say that if you pinch your skin and it doesn't go down you are dehydrated. Whoever wrote that doesn't know the meaning of crêpe.

Forgotten people live in a hole in the ground safe from the world's confusion and chaos.

40   Light shines through the slats
        piercing a thought.

If you were a total zero
I wouldn't be going out with you.
Would you mind increasing
the percentage?

42   How do you take back a fart?

I'll have a hot dog.
I'll get my kicks anyway I can.

44 Are you a comma or
an apostrophe?

Don't talk to me like we're married.   45

46   Poems jump in my head
and pound till I let them out.

Pay attention to me
or I am going to rub your leg.

48 People with husbands have no idea what it's like without one.

You left and my heart crumbled.
I pick up the pieces one at a time.

50

I look you in the eye
while you count sheep.

If you think you know what I'm
thinking and you're wrong it really
fucks up a relationship.

Living life in a cloud of confusion.
Escaping ????

Everybody's there but me, one
comma instead of a period. How
do I make the sentence whole?

54

I am so busy planning the next
party I miss the moment.

Happiness is listening to music
with you in my future.

Laughing together we cruise along
until the next hole in the road.

Never mind what I said.
This is what I meant.

58   I want to crash your life.

Projected face hides
behind a tired mask.

60   The city of impossibility.

I went on a river cruise
for two weeks and during the
entire time I was a secret.

I have enough food
in my teeth for breakfast.

Out of the blue attack.
Don't you know it's hard to
discipline an angel.

Count to 10
then wait for a while
till calm settles in.

The sun came out
the bush turned green
The earth smiled.
People came
technos rained
the earth cried.

A drip of water a point in time
when you are here beside me.

Your face fell away
when you slept next door.

I sat on a flower and grew.

A dog chasing a bone, a rabbit,
a carrot, scratching in the dirt
we seek.

I never look at the stars anymore.

On an Air Force Base watching planes dropping bombs reminds me of the bluebird of happiness flying over your birthday cake.

Why do I let myself drift away?

God said he's my pain in the ass.

74   Stick with me
I'll take care of the crumbs.

How was your vacation?
Well the toilet overflowed on the
last night. That about describes it.

My lyrics are better than
the lyrics of life.

How do I love thee?   77
Let me count the ways:
funny attractive sexy smart.

If I pretend we're married
the barbs roll off my back.

When you look at me
smile with your eyes
your lopsided grin shows
no gladness.

If you have to wear a mask make
sure you bring breath mints.

When can we talk about nothing
meaningful except maybe you?

A text does not fill the silence.

Time drips down the wall, its
bloody trail trapping us inside.

You might think you will live forever
but I know I won't so shape up.

I have gotten extremely
friendly with yams lately.

86   When I hear from you
my world rights itself.

When you threw me away
a little tiny piece of me stayed
inside. Oh the havoc I will make.

88   Good times flash before my eyes;
togetherness dies

A celebratory cheer for all who are here.

A hand peeked over the horizon
new day
new beginnings.

www.ingramcontent.com/pod-product-compliance
Lightning Source LLC
Chambersburg PA
CBHW071237090426
42736CB00014B/3122